MEMOIRS
Of A
JEWELER

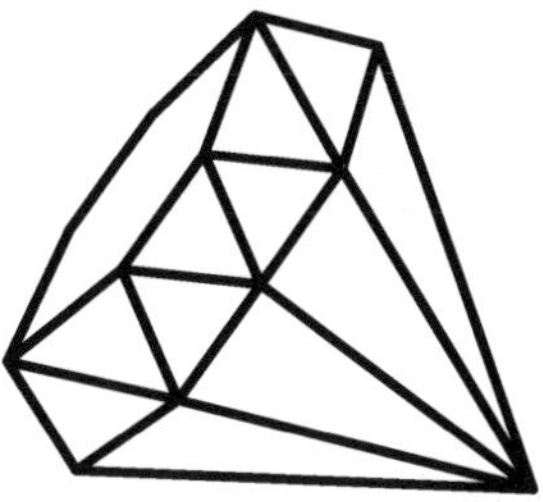

I MADE WOMEN HAPPY AND I GOT MEN OUT OF TROUBLE

BY

ALLAN ABRAMOWITZ

Published by Live Limitless Media Group

Publishing@sierrarainge.com

info@livelimitlessmedia.com

Allan Abramowitz Contact Information:

Email: allanstuart1953@gmail.com

Printed in the United States of America

ISBN: 978-1-952903-72-4

Library of Congress Registration Number

TABLE OF

CONTENTS

DEDICATION

To Molly, my loyal companion,
who gives me unconditional love every single day.

Your presence reminds me that true love is
simple, pure, and constant.

For all those who stood behind me in
good times and bad and some that didn't.

INTRODUCTION

"I guarantee the ring, not the marriage."

For decades, master jeweler and gemologist Allan Abramowitz has been the silent witness to life's most cherished and dramatic moments—engagements, anniversaries, apologies, and last-ditch efforts to make things right. From behind the gleaming glass counters of his jewelry store, he has helped countless men choose the perfect ring, watching as love stories unfolded before him—some joyful, others bittersweet.

In *Memoirs of a Jeweler*, Abramowitz shares a collection of heartfelt, humorous, and sometimes heartbreaking tales from his years in the business. Through his expert eye, he distinguishes between couples truly in love and those swept up in the sparkle of materialism. With wit and wisdom, he offers a rare glimpse into the power, pressure, and promise that a small velvet box can hold.

Whether you're a romantic at heart, a skeptic of love, or simply fascinated by the stories behind life's biggest purchases, this book is a captivating journey through the highs and lows of love, commitment, and the fine art of choosing the perfect ring.

A must-read for jewelry lovers, hopeless romantics, and anyone who's ever wondered what really happens when you step up to the counter.

People often ask me, “How did you begin in the jewelry industry?” The truth? It was a twist of fate. I was looking for a job and found a career. I tell people I paid too much—learning through years of experience, mistakes, and a few kind people who showed me the way. There were also a few who misled me, and in doing so, they unknowingly gave me the tools to make a living. More importantly, I’ve impacted generations of men and women who remember me not just for the jewelry I sold them, but for the advice, patience, and guidance I gave them during some of the most important moments of their lives.

Most people think they are just making a purchase when they step into a jewelry store. I tell them they’re crossing a milestone in their lives. Regardless of the size of the purchase, it’s a commitment—to love, to honor, to trust. Jewelry isn’t just about adornment; it’s about marking life’s moments. Engagement rings, birthday gifts, anniversary presents, or even a "just because" piece—more times than not, these purchases come from the heart. And for over 40 years, I've had the privilege of witnessing love in all its forms.

I've often joked with friends and family when they say, "You're a jeweler." I tell them, "No, I'm a psychiatrist." People come in thinking they're just buying a ring, and before they know it, they're telling me about their lives, their relationships, their hopes, and their fears. It's a position of trust and confidence in a unique career. I've been in this business long enough to have sold engagement rings to men whose fathers I sold wedding bands to decades before. It's a full-circle experience, and it's been incredibly rewarding.

As you read these stories, I hope you shed a tear, maybe even smile. These are stories of love and life—the unforgettable, the heartbreaking, the hilarious, and the beautiful moments that come through my store.

CHAPTER
ONE

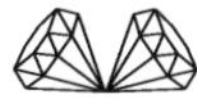

THE REALITY CHECK

I was new to Dallas, Texas, recently relocated by a national jewelry company to assist in opening a store. This was an entirely new experience for me. Born and raised in New York City, I knew nothing about Texas or the South. I had been managing a store in Queens Plaza Mall when this opportunity came up, and I decided to make the move.

The store opened in the early spring, and I had been there about a month when a young man walked in on a quiet weekday morning. The mall had just opened at 10 AM, and he came in immediately, likely our first customer of the day. Most of the staff was still setting up, so I greeted him personally.

He was hard to miss—6’10”, skinny as a beanpole, and barely out of his early twenties. He approached me with an earnestness that caught my attention.

“My name is John,” he said. “I’m looking to get engaged, and I have $200 to spend.”

I smiled. “That’s wonderful, John. I’m going to help you.”

National retail jewelers have a modest inventory, and my store was no different. I led him over to the engagement ring showcase, where we displayed our solitaire rings—yellow gold, white gold, round diamonds, classic designs. The largest diamond in the case was a half-carat, but John’s eyes went straight to the first ring in the row—a simple 1/10 carat diamond in white gold.

I took the ring out of the case and handed it to him. His hands trembled as he examined it, his eyes widening with excitement. A smile stretched across his face as he looked at me and said, “Allan, I love it. I’ll take it.”

“Wait a minute, John. I only showed you one ring.”

He nodded confidently. “I love it. She’ll love it.”

I chuckled. “What’s her name?”

“Susie.”

“How long have you known Susie?”

“A little over a year.”

“Does she know you’re planning to propose?”

John shook his head, grinning. “Nope. She has no idea.”

I loved his enthusiasm. He reached into his pocket, pulling out small bills—fives and tens—and carefully counted out his money. I took the ring to the back, cleaned it, placed it in a beautiful box, and brought it back to John at the counter. He was smiling from ear to ear, practically bouncing on his feet.

He shook my hand firmly. "Thank you so much for helping me," he said before walking out, his heart full and his mind set on forever.

The Moment That Changed Everything

A week passed, and the following Saturday, as I supervised the store, I caught sight of him again. John was impossible to miss, towering over the crowd. But this time, he wasn't alone.

Susie, the lucky girl, was with him. She was a petite blonde, barely 4'10" and maybe 100 pounds soaking wet, with bright blue eyes. I noticed immediately—her cheeks were beet red, and tears streamed down her face.

I looked up and whispered, *God, you're going to help me, right?*

They approached the counter, John holding the small blue jewelry bag in his hands. My heart clenched for a moment—was something wrong? Then I saw the joy in Susie's eyes, and I knew.

John had proposed. And she had said yes.

She was still crying. "It's too big," she said, holding up her hand, the ring loose on her delicate finger. "I need to have it resized."

John beamed. "She hasn't stopped crying since last night."

At that moment, I realized something important—love isn't measured by the size of the diamond. John and Susie's love story wasn't about the price tag, the carat weight, or what anyone else thought. It was about them, about the simple, pure joy of knowing you've found your person.

That was one of the most beautiful proposals I had ever witnessed—not because of the ring, but because of the love it represented.

LOVE GEM

"The value of love isn't measured in carats—it's measured in commitment."

CHAPTER
TWO

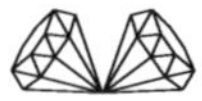

THE FEAR OF REJECTION

Robert was a senior at SMU University in Dallas, Texas, studying business. He had been dating Michelle since their freshman year, and as they approached graduation, talk of marriage became more frequent. He knew he wanted to spend his life with her, and he had spent the last four years saving up for an engagement ring.

By the time he stepped into my store one sunny Saturday morning, he had accumulated about $5,000—a substantial amount for a college student. He was proud of his savings and had no intention of overextending himself. He wanted to do this the right way, on his own.

When Robert and Michelle walked in, I could see the excitement in his eyes. He was ready. I greeted them at the door, and Robert quickly told me what they were there for. Helping young couples just starting their journey was one of the things I loved most about my job. It had been the foundation of my career, and even now, decades later, it still gave me the same satisfaction.

Michelle led the way as we looked through the engagement rings. We went through various styles and different shaped diamonds. Robert had an idea of what he wanted, and as we moved through the options, one ring stood out—a timeless, classic design. Michelle admired it, and Robert looked at me and said, “I think that’s the one.”

I smiled as I measured Michelle’s finger and started processing the transaction. Robert was beaming, ready to take the next step in their journey together.

Then, just as I was finalizing the details, Michelle’s voice cut through the air.

“Allan, wait a minute.”

Robert, who had been sitting next to her, turned to look at her, surprised. “What’s wrong?” I asked.

Michelle sighed and glanced at the ring. “I can’t wear that diamond,” she said, her voice flat. “It’s too small. My sorority sisters would laugh at me.”

Time seemed to stop. I looked at Robert, and I watched the blood drain from his face. His hands, which had been steady just moments ago, clenched into fists on the table. His eyes, once filled with hope, became glassy, his entire body stiff with shock. It was as if someone had sucker-punched him.

I sat there, equally stunned.

I cleared my throat and looked at Michelle. “Robert loves this ring. He’s giving it to you from his heart. He has saved this money over the last four years to prepare for this moment.”

Michelle shook her head. “I just can’t,” she said, crossing her arms. “It’s too small.”

I stopped typing the receipt. The room fell into silence.

Robert stood up slowly, still in shock. He turned to me and said, “I’m sorry to have wasted your time.”

Without another word, he walked toward the door. Michelle hesitated for a moment before following him out. As the door closed behind them, I took a deep breath and looked up at the ceiling.

God, please don’t let him marry that girl.

I never heard from them again.

The Weight of Expectation

The fear of rejection looms large over men when they walk into my store. For many, it's not just about the money—it's about proving their love in a way that will be accepted. Society tells them that a bigger diamond equals a greater love, but when did love become about impressing outsiders rather than cherishing the person you're committing to?

I've seen men agonize over their choices, second-guessing every decision, terrified that they'll pick the "wrong" ring and face rejection. It's heartbreaking. A man can stand at the counter, pouring his heart into his decision, and all it takes is one dismissive comment to shatter his confidence.

I always tell couples this: If the love is real, the size of the diamond doesn't matter. The ring isn't about validation—it's about commitment. If you're more worried about what your friends will say than about the love you share, maybe the problem isn't the ring.

Robert deserved someone who appreciated his effort, not just the carat weight. Wherever he is, I hope he found that person.

LOVE GEM

"A man's love is not measured by the size of the diamond but by the depth of his devotion."

CHAPTER THREE

JACK & PATTY'S 40TH ANNIVERSARY

Jack was the CEO of a major corporation in Dallas, now retired. He had built a successful career, providing his family with everything they needed and more. But there was one thing he hadn't done—upgrade Patty's engagement ring. After 39 years of marriage, their 40th anniversary was approaching, and Jack was ready to celebrate the woman who had been by his side through it all.

One afternoon, Jack walked into my store with Patty by his side. I was standing near the entrance when they arrived, and I greeted them warmly. Jack spoke first, his voice calm yet firm. “Our anniversary is coming up, and I want to buy Patty a new ring.”

Patty glanced down at her left hand, where she wore a simple yellow gold solitaire with a one-carat round diamond—the same ring Jack had given her all those years ago. She shook her head and protested immediately.

“Jack, I don’t need a new ring.”

“Jack, I love my ring.”

“Jack, why are you spending all this money?”

This went on for over an hour. We looked at different diamonds, shapes, and designs while Patty voiced her disapproval. Meanwhile, Jack stood quietly in the corner, listening, letting her talk, saying very little. He didn't argue, didn't push—just observed. But I could see the determination in his eyes.

Finally, I couldn't take it anymore. I turned to Patty and said, "Patty, listen to me. This ring is not for you. It's for Jack."

She looked at me, confused. "What do you mean?"

I took a breath. "Jack told me you have three children."

She nodded. "Yes, I do."

"He told me you have five grandchildren."

Patty smiled. "Yes, I do."

"He told me you've been married for 39 years, and your 40th anniversary is coming up."

Her expression softened. "That's right."

I met her gaze and said, "Jack wants to buy you a ring. Let him buy you a ring."

She was silent for a moment, then turned to look at Jack. He didn't say a word—he didn't need to. He had already made up his mind. And in that instant, Patty understood.

Jack purchased a stunning seven-carat oval diamond set in a custom-designed platinum ring. It was beautiful, timeless—just like their love.

Months later, around Christmas, Patty returned to the store to have her ring cleaned. As I handed it back to her, she smiled and kissed me on the cheek.

"I get it now," she said softly. "It really was for Jack."

LOVE GEM

"Sometimes, a gift isn't about what you need—it's about what someone needs to give."

CHAPTER FOUR

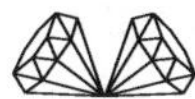

PRETENTIOUS LOVE

Tim and Carol had been dating for several years, both focused on building their careers. They had finally reached a point where marriage was the next step, and they wandered into my store one weekday to begin the engagement ring shopping process.

Carol had a very particular taste—she loved round-cut diamonds because of how much they sparkled. Tim, eager to make her happy, was willing to buy her whatever she wanted. He had been working at his first job out of college for a few years and had managed to save up for this moment.

We explored different styles and sizes, and while some of the larger diamonds were beyond Tim's budget, they eventually settled on something classic, elegant, and within reach. A white gold solitaire with a beautiful round-cut diamond. Carol seemed thrilled, and Tim beamed as he pulled out his credit card to make the purchase.

It was a seamless transaction, nothing complicated. I printed the receipt, shook their hands, and they left, excited for the future.

Or so I thought.

A few days later, the store had just opened for the day when I saw Carol walk through the door alone. She waved and smiled as she approached me. I greeted her warmly, assuming she was here for a routine visit.

"Allan, can I talk to you for a minute?" she asked.

"Of course," I said, leading her into my office.

She took a seat, her expression calm, almost casual. Then she got straight to the point. "Do you remember the larger diamond you showed Tim and me? Do you still have it?"

I was taken aback for a moment but nodded. "Let me check." I went to the safe and, sure enough, the diamond was still there. When I returned, I placed it in front of her.

"Yes, we still have it," I said.

Without hesitation, she pulled out her credit card and said, "I want it. Change the diamond. He will never know."

I stared at her for a second, trying to process what she had just said. "Carol… are you sure?"

She nodded. "Yes. Tim picked the ring, but I want this diamond. I'll pay for the upgrade myself, and he'll never have to know."

I had seen a lot in my career, but this was one of those moments that stuck with me. This wasn't just about a bigger diamond. This was a glimpse into the way Carol saw marriage—starting it with a secret, with deception.

Tim picked up the ring a few days later, completely unaware of the change. Weeks later, he proposed, and Carol said yes.

A year later, they both came back to purchase wedding bands. As I handed them their rings, I glanced at Tim, wondering if he had any idea that the diamond Carol wore wasn't the one he had chosen for her. To this day, I don't believe he ever knew.

Some relationships begin with trust. Others begin with illusion.

LOVE GEM

"A strong relationship is built on trust, not deception."

CHAPTER
FIVE

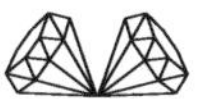

TO LOVE AND TO LOSE

Michael was beginning his freshman year of high school when he first saw Karen. It was the first day of school, and as he wandered from class to class, trying to get his bearings in an unfamiliar building, he found himself in the cafeteria at lunchtime. He sat alone, scanning the room, overwhelmed by the new faces. Then, out of the corner of his eye, he saw her.

Karen was sitting with her friends, laughing, her eyes bright. Something about her caught his attention, and for the rest of the lunch period, he barely touched his food. He didn't know what it was—her smile, the way she tucked her hair behind her ear, the way she seemed completely at ease. But in that moment, he knew he wanted to get to know her.

The next day, he walked into a class he hadn't attended yet and immediately noticed Karen sitting in the back of the room. His heart fluttered, and he stole glances at her throughout the lesson, barely registering what the teacher was saying. When the bell rang, he saw her gathering her things, and before he could stop himself, he walked up to her.

"Hi," he said nervously. "My name is Michael. What's your name?"

Karen smiled. “I’m Karen.”

That was the beginning.

They became inseparable. Friday night football games, weekend movies, long walks around town. As the months passed, their bond grew deeper. They weren’t just boyfriend and girlfriend—they were best friends. They talked about everything, from their dreams for the future to their fears about growing up.

By the time high school ended, they had spent four years together. When Karen left for college out of state, they promised they’d make it work. They wrote letters, made phone calls, visited each other when they could. But as time went on, the distance became harder. Their lives were pulling them in different directions, and eventually, they had to make the painful decision to let each other go.

Years passed. Michael built a career, got married, had children. But every so often, he would think about Karen. The way she laughed. The way she made him feel like the most important person in the world. First loves have a way of staying with you, no matter how much time passes.

One afternoon, decades later, Michael walked into my store. He had come in looking for an anniversary gift for his wife. As we talked, he glanced down at a display of engagement rings and smiled.

“You know,” he said, his voice distant, “I once bought a ring for a girl I never got to propose to.”

I raised an eyebrow. “Really?”

He nodded. “Karen. She was my high school sweetheart. I saved up for months to buy her a ring, but before I could propose, life took us in different directions.”

“What happened to the ring?” I asked.

He chuckled. "I kept it for years, but eventually, I let it go. I realized I had been holding onto a memory, not a future."

Michael bought a beautiful necklace for his wife that day. As he left, I saw him pause at the door, looking back at the engagement rings one last time. Then he smiled to himself and walked away.

Some love stories don't end the way we expect them to. Some are meant to shape us, to teach us, to remind us of what it means to feel deeply. And sometimes, love isn't about holding on—it's about knowing when to let go.

LOVE GEM

"Some love stories end, but the memories remain timeless."

CHAPTER
SIX

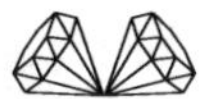

WE CAN'T MAKE THIS SH*T UP

Over the years, I've learned that no two love stories are the same. Some are filled with joy, some with heartbreak, and some… well, some are so outrageous that even I couldn't make them up if I tried.

One afternoon, a man rushed into my store, out of breath, looking around as if someone was chasing him. He leaned over the counter and whispered, "I need a diamond. Fast."

I raised an eyebrow. "Alright… What's the occasion?"

He ran a hand through his hair, visibly stressed. "I messed up—bad."

Now, in my line of work, I've seen a lot of men in panic mode. Some are nervous about proposing, others have waited until the last minute for an anniversary gift. But this guy? This guy was different. He was sweating bullets.

I guided him over to the engagement rings. "Tell me what happened."

He exhaled sharply. "I was supposed to propose last night, had this whole thing planned out… but I lost the ring."

I paused. "You lost it?"

He nodded, looking around as if someone might hear. "I had a poker game with the guys, had a few drinks, and somehow—somehow—I bet the ring."

I blinked. "You bet the engagement ring?"

He put his hands up. "It wasn't supposed to happen! It was a stupid bet! And then I lost!"

At this point, I was just trying not to laugh. "Does she know?"

He shook his head. "No! But she's expecting a proposal tonight, and I have to replace it before she finds out."

I sighed, grabbed a ring that was similar in size and shape to what he described, and handed it to him. "Here. This should do the trick."

He looked at it, then at me. "You're saving my life."

I smirked. "Yeah, well, maybe lay off the poker tables for a while."

The Unexpected Proposal

Then there was the time a man planned an elaborate, romantic proposal in a hot air balloon. He came into my store, excited, picking out the perfect ring. He had everything set—sunset ride, champagne, a photographer waiting to capture the moment when he got down on one knee.

The morning after the proposal, he walked back into my store looking… not so thrilled.

I greeted him, curious. “How’d it go?”

He ran a hand over his face. “She said yes.”

“That’s great!”

He shook his head. “Yeah, except I dropped the ring.”

I froze. “You *what*?”

“The ring. Slipped right out of my hand. It fell from 1,500 feet in the air.”

I stared at him. “So, it’s… gone?”

He sighed. "Oh yeah. It's gone. Somewhere in a field. Or maybe a lake. Who knows?"

I chuckled. "Well, I take it that's why you're here?"

He nodded. "Yeah. We need a new one. Preferably one that stays on my damn hand."

Some stories make you laugh, some make you shake your head, and some make you question how certain people survive in life. But at the end of the day, love is unpredictable. It's messy, it's chaotic, and sometimes, it's downright ridiculous. But that's what makes it so great.

I've seen men propose in the most extravagant ways, and I've seen them get down on one knee in my store's parking lot because they just couldn't wait another second. At the end of the day, the ring is just a piece of the story—the real magic is in the love behind it.

LOVE GEM

"Love is unpredictable, but the right one is undeniable."

CHAPTER
SEVEN

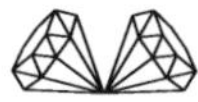

MAKE IT LAST FOREVER

If there's one thing I've learned after decades in the jewelry business, it's that love isn't about the grand gestures. It's about the commitment to making it last. I've met couples who have been together for decades, who have weathered storms, built families, and stood by each other through thick and thin. Their secret? Love is a daily choice, not just an emotion.

One of my favorite customers, Mr. and Mrs. Thompson, were one such couple. They had been married for fifty-five years when they walked into my store, hand in hand, like two young lovers. Mrs. Thompson had lost her original engagement ring while gardening decades ago, and Mr. Thompson had promised that one day, he would replace it.

He finally did—on their fifty-fifth anniversary.

As I handed her the ring, tears welled in her eyes. She looked at her husband and whispered, "I'd say yes all over again."

I watched as he kissed her forehead and squeezed her hand. It was a moment that reminded me of why I do what I do. Rings don't just symbolize a promise; they represent a lifetime of choices, moments, and memories.

The Foundation of Forever

Not every love story lasts, but the ones that do have common threads—patience, understanding, and a willingness to grow together. I've had men walk into my store to replace lost rings, upgrade diamonds, or simply buy a new band because their fingers have changed over the years. But what stands out to me the most are the couples who come in together, still choosing each other after decades.

One day, an elderly gentleman named Walter came into the store alone. His wife of sixty years had recently passed away, and he stood before me, holding her wedding band in his trembling hands. "I just want to have it resized," he said softly. "So I can wear it."

We resized the ring and made it into a necklace for him, so he could keep her close to his heart. As he left, he smiled and said, "She was the love of my life. And she still is."

That's what making it last forever means. Love doesn't end—it simply changes form.

LOVE GEM

"True love isn't about finding someone perfect—it's about choosing someone perfectly, every single day."

CHAPTER
EIGHT

TECHNOLOGY VS. TRADITION—HAS LOVE LOST ITS SPARK?

Love used to be about handwritten letters, late-night phone calls, and waiting weeks to see someone again. Now, with a single swipe, a person can meet their next potential soulmate—or their next temporary distraction.

Technology has changed the way people date, communicate, and even propose. Some of these changes have been for the better, but many have eroded the emotional depth that relationships once thrived on.

In both my business and personal life, I've seen a shift—one that concerns me. Society has become emotionally disconnected. People hide behind texts, emails, and unread messages rather than face real conversations.

I see it in relationships. I see it in business. And if we're being honest, we all feel it.

The Ghosting Epidemic

There was a time when a breakup required a conversation. When relationships—romantic or otherwise—ended, people had to face each other. Now? People just disappear.

One of my longtime customers, James, had been dating a woman for over a year. He was ready to propose. He came into my store, picked out the ring, and was planning the perfect moment. Then, one day, she just… stopped responding.

Calls went unanswered. Texts were left on read. No fight. No warning. Just silence.

Ghosting isn't just happening in relationships—it's happening in business, in friendships, in life. Rather than confronting problems, people vanish. It's easier to avoid than to address.

And this emotional disconnection isn't just about avoiding awkward conversations—it's changing the way we treat people.

We live in an era where people would rather send a quick text than make a phone call. A conversation that could be resolved in five minutes now drags out over hours or even days. But what's worse? People have stopped addressing real issues altogether.

I've seen it in my own business. A client will ask for something, I'll fulfill the request, and then when it's time to finalize, suddenly they're unreachable. No explanation, no response—just gone.

It's not just about avoiding payments—it's about avoiding accountability.

The same way people ghost each other in relationships, they do it in business. They dodge responsibility. They disappear instead of resolving conflicts.

It's a commentary on our times, and I believe it's important to talk about. Relationships—both personal and professional—aren't meant to be disposable.

Bringing Back Real Connection

Technology is a tool, not a replacement for real effort. The strongest relationships—whether in love or in business—are built on communication, trust, and accountability.

Here's how we change things:

- Have real conversations. Stop hiding behind texts and emails. Call. Meet in person. Look people in the eye.
- Address issues head-on. If a relationship isn't working, if a deal isn't closing, if something needs to be said—say it.
- Stop ghosting. If you don't want to continue something, have the courage to be honest. People deserve clarity, even when it's uncomfortable.
- Remember, people matter. We are more than usernames, profiles, and text bubbles. We are human beings with real emotions, real needs, and real connections to maintain.

At the end of the day, love, business, and life itself require emotional investment. No amount of technology can replace that.

LOVE GEM

"Love, respect, and accountability should never be replaced by convenience."

CHAPTER
NINE

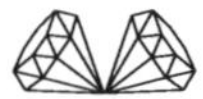

THE LEGACY OF LOVE-RINGS AS TIMELESS ASSETS

A ring is more than metal and stone. It carries history, emotions, and a legacy that extends far beyond the person wearing it. Some rings mark the beginning of a love story, while others serve as cherished reminders of the past.

I've had the honor of selling engagement rings, anniversary gifts, and heirloom-quality pieces that families intend to pass down for generations. And what I've learned is this: jewelry isn't just a possession—it's a legacy.

The Ring That Carried a Century of Love

One of my most memorable customers was an elderly man named Walter. He walked into my store, slow but steady, clutching a small box in his wrinkled hands.

"I need this cleaned," he said, handing it to me.

Inside was an antique diamond ring, its band slightly worn, but its beauty timeless.

"This ring belonged to my grandmother," he continued. "She passed it to my mother on her wedding day, and my mother gave it to my wife when we got married. Now, it's my granddaughter's turn."

I held the ring carefully, struck by the weight of its history. Four generations of love, all tied to this single piece of jewelry.

Walter wasn't just giving his granddaughter a ring—he was giving her a symbol of the love, strength, and commitment that had been passed down through their family for over a century.

When I returned the ring to him, polished and gleaming, he smiled. "It's not about the diamonds," he said. "It's about the love that never fades."

Why Heirloom Jewelry Holds More Value Than Any Appraisal

I've seen people sell engagement rings after breakups. I've also seen people treasure rings that belonged to their great-grandparents, holding onto them as priceless pieces of family history.

Financially, jewelry is an asset—it retains value and can be passed down, sold, or repurposed. But emotionally, its worth is immeasurable.

- A wedding ring from a grandmother becomes a symbol of enduring love.
- A father's cufflinks become a reminder of strength and tradition.
- A necklace gifted by a mother carries memories of wisdom and care.

Unlike money, which can be spent, or houses, which can change hands, jewelry remains. It tells a story. It connects generations.

Many cultures believe in the tradition of passing down wedding rings, engagement stones, and other significant pieces of jewelry.

I've seen families come in together, a grandmother handing a ring to her grandson, a father placing his late wife's bracelet into the hands of his daughter. There's a reverence in those moments—a silent acknowledgment that love doesn't end when life does.

Even in business, I've had customers return to my store decades later, bringing their children and grandchildren to buy their own engagement rings. "This is where my father bought my mother's ring," they say. "It only feels right to buy mine here too."

That's the power of legacy.

Jewelry as an Investment in Love and Wealth

While jewelry is often seen as sentimental, it's also one of the smartest financial assets a person can own. Unlike cars that depreciate, high-quality jewelry retains and even increases in value over time.

A well-crafted diamond ring can be worn for a lifetime and still be worth more decades later.

Some customers buy jewelry with investment in mind—choosing timeless, high-quality pieces that can be passed down while maintaining their monetary worth. Others buy with heart in mind, knowing that no matter what happens, the value of the ring is in the love it represents.

Either way, jewelry is one of the few things in life that holds both financial and emotional significance.

I once asked a longtime married couple what their rings meant to them after 50 years together. The husband smiled and said, "It reminds me that love, like gold, only gets stronger over time."

That's what jewelry is. It's not just a possession—it's a story. A promise. A legacy.

And when it's passed down, it carries more than just its original meaning. It carries love from one generation to the next.

LOVE GEM

"A true legacy isn't what you leave behind—it's what you pass forward."

CHAPTER
TEN

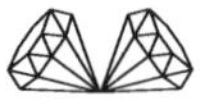

WHAT LOVE TAUGHT ME

After more than forty years in the jewelry business, I've sold thousands of engagement rings, anniversary gifts, and "just because" pieces. I've met people in every phase of love—excited young couples, anxious husbands, skeptical fiancées, and occasionally, heartbroken partners looking for closure. From behind the counter, I've witnessed the best and worst of relationships, and through those encounters, I've learned more about love than I ever imagined I would.

What love has taught me is that it's not a straight path. It's messy. It's complicated. It's wildly unpredictable. But it's also beautiful.

Love is quiet more often than loud. The loud gestures—the roses, the dinner proposals, the Instagram-worthy surprises—are lovely. But it's the quiet acts of love that I've come to cherish the most. I've watched men spend their entire paycheck on a modest diamond, just to see the smile on her face. I've seen women cry when they hold a ring—not because it was extravagant, but because it reminded them of a grandmother or a promise made years ago.

I've learned that love has nothing to do with carat size. I've watched customers with large budgets struggle to pick out a ring because they were chasing perfection. And I've seen broke college students walk out of my store with a $200 ring that meant more than any six-figure stone. The sincerity in their eyes? That's what made it priceless.

I've seen love tested. I remember the man who returned to upgrade a ring he had bought during hard times. He told me, "She never complained. She just smiled and wore it like it was the Hope Diamond. Now that I can, I want to give her the ring she deserves." That's love.

I've also seen love walk away. The engagements that never happened. The wedding bands returned with trembling hands and broken hearts. I remember one woman who brought back her ring and said, "We grew apart. But I wanted you to know you helped me believe in something real. Even if it didn't last forever."

Love has taught me that people aren't always looking for a piece of jewelry—they're looking for hope. They're looking for reassurance that what they feel is real, and they come into my store hoping that the ring will somehow make it all come together.

Some days, I've felt like a therapist more than a jeweler. And honestly? I've been honored to be that person. People have shared their fears, their mistakes, their dreams—and I've listened.

I've learned that timing matters. That forgiveness is hard. That people love differently, but we all want the same thing: to feel chosen.

So if you ask me what love has taught me after all these years, I'll say this:

Love is not perfect. But when it's true—it endures. It adapts. It survives.

The jewelry may fade. The sparkle may dull. But the stories? The stories stay with me. Every day.

LOVE GEM

"The most valuable gems aren't set in rings—they're found in the hearts we choose to love."

CHAPTER
ELEVEN

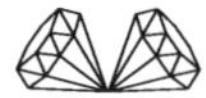

LESSONS IN LOVE

Over the years, I've had a front-row seat to some of the greatest lessons in love—not because I went looking for them, but because they walked through my door. Some came in tears, some came in joy, and many walked out changed. And so did I.

I've seen what patience looks like in love. One couple—married over 50 years—came in to upgrade their rings. They had been through everything together: loss, illness, raising kids, starting over. The husband said, "This isn't a new ring, it's a thank-you. For sticking with me through all the mess." Patience like that doesn't come in pretty packaging—it's earned, and it's real.

I've learned that communication saves relationships. One day, a young couple came in arguing about what ring to buy. You could feel the tension. I quietly stepped back and let them talk. After a while, they realized they weren't really arguing about the ring—they were afraid. Afraid of making a mistake. Afraid of commitment. When they stopped talking at each other and started listening, everything changed. They picked a ring together. I still remember how tightly she held his hand.

Another lesson? Know who you are before trying to love someone else. I saw a man call off his engagement days before the wedding. Not because he didn't love her, but because he didn't love himself enough to show up fully in the relationship. That kind of honesty is rare—and brave. Love isn't about being perfect. It's about being ready.

I've watched people choose love again after heartbreak. A widow came in, quiet and composed, looking for a new piece—not to replace what was lost, but to carry it forward. "He'd want me to be happy," she told me. "And this ring is a reminder that I still am."

I've also seen when love needs space. I once helped a couple choose an engagement ring. A year later, they returned—to return it. Not because they didn't care, but because they realized they were better apart. There was no bitterness, just mutual respect. Sometimes, love teaches you to let go.

And perhaps the biggest lesson? Love is active. It's not just something you feel—it's something you choose, every single day. In a world that changes constantly, love asks for presence, grace, and effort. I've seen that in every man who saved up for months to buy a modest ring. In every woman who said, "It's not about the size, it's about the meaning."

These aren't fairy tales. They're real-life stories from real people. And the lessons stay with me.

Love is patient. Love is work. Love is sometimes messy, often magical, and always worth the risk.

LOVE GEM

"Love doesn't just happen. It's chosen, protected, and nurtured—every single day."

CHAPTER
TWELVE

BEFORE YOU SAY 'I DO'

There's a certain stillness in the moments before someone proposes. The hesitation, the heartbeat, the hope. Over the years, I've helped hundreds of people choose the ring that asks the biggest question of their lives: Will you marry me?

But beyond the sparkle of the stone and the thrill of the moment, there's something deeper that lingers in the air—questions that go unspoken, truths that matter more than the carat size.

Before you say "I do," consider this:

Do you like each other when no one's watching? That's the part most people forget. You can love someone deeply but not enjoy who they are day to day. I've seen couples who look great on paper—and terrible in person. Chemistry matters, but compatibility lasts.

Are you aligned on values? Not goals. Values. Do you agree on how to fight, how to forgive, how to handle money, how to raise kids (if you want them), how to respect boundaries? These are the things that don't show up in the honeymoon phase—but they make or break a marriage.

Are you ready to give more than you take? Marriage isn't 50/50—it's 100/100. You both have to be willing to show up, even when the other person can't. Especially then.

One of my favorite stories comes from a couple who bought a modest ring. The woman looked at her fiancé and said, "You're the best decision I've ever made." He smiled and said, "You're the best responsibility I've ever had." That stuck with me. Love is emotional—but marriage is a responsibility. A beautiful one, yes, but a responsibility nonetheless.

Before you say "I do," ask yourself: do I trust this person with my silence, my fears, my dreams? Can I fail in front of them? Can I be vulnerable and know they'll protect me, not shame me?

And more importantly—can I do that for them?

Rings are a symbol. But the promise? That's what matters most.

So if you're getting ready to propose or walk down the aisle, take a deep breath. Look at the person in front of you. And know that while the ring might shine, it's your actions that will make it last.

LOVE GEM

"Before you say 'I do,' make sure you already have."

CHAPTER THIRTEEN

A DAY IN THE LIFE AT THE DIAMOND DISTRICT

There was nothing quite like the pulse of New York City's Diamond District in the 1980s. It was a world within a world—fast, intense, electric. Every morning on 47th Street, the city would hum to life as metal gates opened, storefront lights flickered on, and diamond dealers carried coffee in one hand and locked briefcases in the other. This was where I built my business, where I built my reputation, and where I earned my place in the world of jewelry.

Running Odyssey Jewelers wasn't just a job—it was a lifestyle. My day often began before the sun was up. I'd arrive at the shop early, sometimes catching the tail end of overnight deliveries. Security was everything. We worked behind bulletproof glass. Cameras watched every angle. We kept our showcases spotless, our vaults secure, and our relationships tighter than any clasp on a necklace.

Customers ranged from tourists and couples to celebrities and wholesale buyers. Everyone wanted a deal. And everyone thought they knew more than they did. But that was the beauty of it—educating them, helping them see the value, the quality, the story behind each piece.

One morning, a young man came in with his father. They were nervous, you could tell. The father nodded for the son to speak. "I'm here to buy an engagement ring," the son said. "But I don't want my girlfriend to know how much it cost."

I smiled. "Most people don't."

We spent hours going through designs. The father reminisced about the first ring he bought for his wife—right there in the same district, decades earlier. That day, I wasn't just selling a ring—I was bridging two generations with one decision.

Some days were glamorous, like when celebrities came in under aliases, wearing sunglasses and hats. Other days were intense—customers haggling hard, competitors trying to outbid one another, tension thick in the air. We'd close deals in whispers, often with just a handshake and a look.

And of course, there was the TV show—*The Cable Jeweler*. We filmed in a small studio space, featuring our inventory, interviewing suppliers, and educating people about stones and settings. It was grassroots marketing before social media ever existed. And people watched. People called. People came in because they saw me on screen and felt like they already knew me.

The Diamond District was raw and real. You had to be sharp, but you also had to have heart. Because while the business was built on sparkle, the real value was built on trust.

Looking back, I'm grateful for every long day, every difficult customer, every handshake, every story. The Diamond District didn't just teach me how to be a jeweler—it taught me how to be a professional, a confidant, a part of people's most meaningful moments.

LOVE GEM

"In the Diamond District, every deal is a story—and every story begins with trust."

FIND YOUR PERFECT ENGAGEMENT RING QUIZ

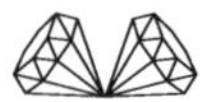

Not sure what ring best suits your love story?
Answer these fun questions to find the perfect style!

1. What describes your partner best?

   a) Classic and timeless

   b) Bold and adventurous

   c) Romantic and sentimental

   d) Chic and modern

2. If your partner were a gemstone, which one would they be?

   a) Diamond – timeless and strong

   b) Sapphire – deep and mysterious

   c) Emerald – rare and enchanting

   d) Rose gold – unique and stylish

3. What's your ideal proposal setting?

   a) A candlelit dinner at a fancy restaurant

   b) A surprise trip to a breathtaking location

   c) A meaningful, intimate moment at home

   d) A bold, public declaration

Results:

- Mostly A's: A classic solitaire or vintage ring is perfect for your partner. Simple, elegant, and forever stylish.
- Mostly B's: Consider a unique, bold design with a colorful gemstone to match their adventurous personality.
- Mostly C's: An intricate, sentimental setting—perhaps one with a hidden detail or family heirloom—would mean the most.
- Mostly D's: A sleek, modern design with a unique band or setting would be ideal.

THE "HOW WELL DO YOU KNOW YOUR PARTNER?" QUIZ

Test your knowledge and see how well you truly know your significant other!

1. What's their favorite flower?
2. What's their dream vacation spot?
3. What's their go-to comfort food?
4. What's a movie they could watch over and over?
5. If they could meet any celebrity, who would it be?

6. What's a childhood memory they always talk about?
7. What's their biggest pet peeve?
8. What's their favorite way to spend a weekend?

Score Yourself:

- 6-8 correct:

  You know them better than they know themselves!

- 3-5 correct:

  You're doing well, but keep listening and learning.

- 0-2 correct:

  Time to start paying more attention!

Jewelry may sparkle, but it's love that truly shines. Whether you're beginning your journey, building a legacy, or just enjoying the little moments that make love magical, remember: it's not about the size of the diamond—it's about the depth of the love.

In the end I guaranteed the ring but not the marriage. Wishing the best for you.

FINAL LOVE GEM

"Jewelry fades, but love lasts forever."

ABOUT THE AUTHOR

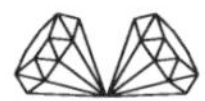

Born and raised in New York City, Allan Abramowitz developed an early appreciation for business and craftsmanship. He earned his **Bachelor of Arts in Political Science** with a minor in **Business Administration** from **American University in Washington, D.C.** in 1973. After graduation, he worked various sales positions in New York and Washington before finding his true calling in the jewelry industry.

In **1978**, he established **Odyssey Jewelers**, a retail jewelry business and manufacturing operation located in **New York City's prestigious Diamond District**. His expertise and entrepreneurial drive led him to become a **member of the Diamond Dealers Club of New York** and, in 1983, he took his passion to television, producing and hosting *The Cable Jeweler*, a public access show that showcased Odyssey Jewelers, industry insights, and interviews with leading jewelry professionals—years before home shopping networks became the norm.

In **1988**, he completed his **Graduate Gemologist (GG) certification from the Gemological Institute of America (GIA)**, solidifying his reputation as an expert in diamonds and fine jewelry. However, his creative pursuits led him away from the industry in **1995**, when he decided to follow another passion—culinary arts. He graduated from the **French Culinary Institute in NYC** in 1997, working as a chef in high-end restaurants and catering businesses. His career expanded into **hotel management**, where he worked as a **Catering Manager and Catering Director** for **Hilton Hotels and The Ritz-Carlton**.

In **2003**, he returned to his first love—jewelry—and began working as a **store manager for Helzberg Diamonds**, taking his talents to **Florida, New York City, and Dallas, TX**. Over the years, he continued to build his expertise in fine jewelry, luxury sales, and diamond consulting. In **2016**, he joined **Diamonds Direct Dallas**, where he remains today as a **Diamond Consultant and Appraiser**.

With over four decades of experience in the jewelry industry, Allan Abramowitz has helped thousands of clients celebrate love, milestones, and legacy through carefully chosen pieces of jewelry. His memoir, *Memoirs of a Jeweler*, shares the heartfelt, humorous, and unforgettable stories he has collected over the years—proving that a jeweler's job goes far beyond selling diamonds; it's about witnessing the very essence of love.

LOVE NOTES

LOVE NOTES

LOVE NOTES

LOVE NOTES

LOVE NOTES

LOVE NOTES

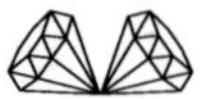

LOVE NOTES

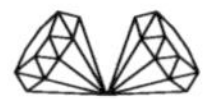

LOVE NOTES

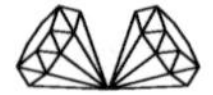

LOVE NOTES

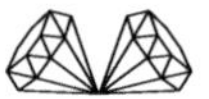

LOVE NOTES

LOVE NOTES

LOVE NOTES

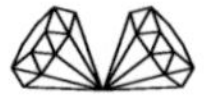

LOVE NOTES

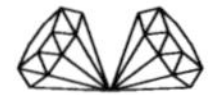